Postcards
from
Heaven

Text and illustrations copyright © Ellie Hart 2016
The author asserts the moral right to be identified as the author of this work

Published by
The Bible Reading Fellowship
15 The Chambers, Vineyard
Abingdon OX14 3FE
United Kingdom
Tel: +44 (0)1865 319700
Email: enquiries@brf.org.uk
Website: www.brf.org.uk
BRF is a Registered Charity

ISBN 978 0 85746 427 9

First published 2016

10 9 8 7 6 5 4 3 2 1 0

Acknowledgements

Unless otherwise stated, scripture quotations are taken from The Holy Bible, New International Version (Anglicised edition) copyright © 1979, 1984, 2011 by Biblica. Used by permission of Hodder & Stoughton Publishers, an Hachette UK company. All rights reserved. 'NIV' is a registered trademark of Biblica. UK trademark number 1448790.

The Living Bible copyright © 1971 by Tyndale House Foundation. Used by permission of Tyndale House Publishers Inc., Carol Stream, Illinois 60188. All rights reserved.

A catalogue record for this book is available from the British Library

Printed and bound by Gutenberg Press, Tarxien, Malta

Postcards
from
Heaven

words and pictures to help you hear from God

Ellie Hart

Some words for the seasons

We all live in a season of one kind or another, a season of work, a season of ministry, a season of looking after children, a season of joy, a season of grieving, seasons of friendship and relationships. The main feature of seasons is that they don't last for ever: the place we move into next may well be different in many ways.

Last summer, a friend of mine who hears God more clearly, perhaps, than anyone else I know came and told me that the Father wanted me to write a book about the seasons that we go through in life, especially about how to get through the tougher seasons and how to navigate those curious empty spaces that come in between seasons of activity.

So I've done my best, and my heart's desire is that this book could become a place where you encounter our wonderful, beautiful, untameable, passionate, loving God and hear him speak directly to you, whatever your circumstances.

When I was a student I moved away from my home in the countryside and went to live in the bustle of a big city. Every time I went home to visit, as I first stepped out of the car I would really notice how clean and fresh the air was. So I'd stop, stand there for a moment and inhale deeply, appreciating it more in that moment than in all the years of growing up.

My hope and prayer are that, for many of you, this book will introduce you to the cool clean air of what God has to say to you and that you will take a moment to breathe it in and feel it refreshing deep parts of your soul.

There isn't just one way to use this book. Some people will flick through the pages until a particular picture catches their attention, and some work through from one end to another. It doesn't matter! But I would suggest that you take time. Sit and think about what the pictures or words mean to you. Talk to God about them and write down what you think you are hearing him say to you. Sometimes I've made a suggestion of something to do or read. God has made us all unique and there are many different ways that we can hear him speak to us. Listen to him the way you know how, and be open to him speaking in new ways.

Above all – breathe deep.
May you be refreshed deep into your soul.
May new life pour into you, through you and out from you.

Be blessed in the name of Jesus. Ellie x

The beginning – who you are

: This instrument is completely beautiful, a piece of art
: in its own right.

: Craftsman made, carefully designed and created with
: a specific task in mind. A piece of art and a piece of
: engineering. Each part is doing a job and the whole is
: tuned and ready.

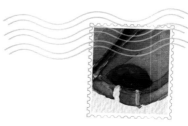

And yet, until it is resting on the shoulder of the master musician and surrendering to the tune that he chooses to play, it cannot achieve its full potential.

So often, we fight back, unable to trust and rest, unwilling to surrender to the tune the master wants to play with our lives. While we are wrestling we are still beautiful, still the work of a master craftsman, still treasured by him. But when we rest on his shoulder and he turns his face to us and lifts his bow – then we become what we were always intended to be.

I rest here on your shoulder,
confident in you,
my maker, my friend.
I rest here on your shoulder,
laying down my right to wield the bow or write the tune.
I rest here
at peace, assured,
knowing that the song you have in mind for me
will be the one my heart was made to sing.

For your journal

Read Psalm 139 and write a response to it.

How do you feel when you say out loud, 'I am fearfully and wonderfully made'?

How easy is it to accept the idea that God knows you better than you know yourself?

Read Proverbs 3:5–6 and write a response to it.

Why do you think we find it hard to trust God, to surrender to him?

What tune might God be wanting to play with your life at the moment?

My mother's bowl

This is my mother's cut glass bowl, filled with sweet pea flowers from her garden. They smell and look beautiful.

The bowl sits on the windowsill in the dining room and nearly always has something in it. Perhaps next time we visit, it will be full of trifle or clementines or loose change, buttons and my mother's car keys. Usually it's something that smells good or brings pleasure, or something that is precious and needs to be kept safe.

There are in-between times, though, when it is cleaned out and polished up and set on the sill with nothing but its own beauty to recommend it – no 'useful' purpose, nothing to 'give' to others, no role. And I've noticed that in those moments, as the light shines in through the window, I can suddenly see its own beauty and the beauty of light caught in cut glass and fractured into a rainbow of colours.

We are so much like this bowl. There are seasons when our lives are filled to overflowing with ministry, mission, family and community. At other times we are called just to be and to let go of our need to do.

What God has been saying to me is that when this bowl is full of flowers, it is not longing for the time when it was brimming with custard! It can live fully in this season, enjoying its joys and enduring its hardships, knowing that one day a new season will come, but that it hasn't come yet.

I search for you:
I strain ahead to look for you,
to see where we will go together,
longing to know, longing to be there –
and I glimpse your face through the mist.
I turn around to look back
at the place where I saw you last –
felt your touch, saw you move –
but the moment has gone.
And yet
when I open my eyes
I see
you are with me now.

For your journal

Think about the season you are currently in and the seasons you have already travelled through.

What were the best things about those past seasons?

What did you learn in each of them?

How would you feel if your current season were to come to an end?

What seasons do you dream of in the future?

How can you see God at work in the season you are walking in now?

In what way can you better embrace the season you are in now?

An invitation

A bench sits in a shady part of the garden. It's a place of peace, rest and friendship. It's a place of quiet and of conversation. It's a place for you to meet with Jesus.

Have you been there lately?

Sometimes I get so busy with life that I forget to retreat into this place of quiet with Jesus. I forget to do the one thing that restores my soul and enables me to keep up the busyness.

Sometimes I'm ashamed that the garden that is my life has become overgrown and messy – so I put off inviting Jesus into it until I've had a chance to tidy it up a bit.

I am so busy trying to make my garden look pretty that I forget to take the time to sit down and have a cup of tea with the master gardener who is waiting for me. How crazy is it that I stand alone, fighting to hack back the weeds with my bare hands, while Jesus stands behind me holding a scythe?

Here's the news: once you've invited God into the garden that is your life, he is always there. He is always ready to sit with you on this bench, to listen to what is on your heart – however ugly it might be – and to speak forgiveness, restoration and love. He already knows about the mess, the corners of brambles and weeds. But his priority, his heart, is to take time to be with you.

And when you make time to sit on that bench, I think he says something like this...

· ·

My friend,
good to see you!
Come, sit down, rest.
My child,
I am so glad you came.
I have so much to tell you,
so much to ask you,
so much to give you.
But first,
my beloved,
take your time –
I have an eternity.
Lean back;
this seat is yours.
Come, sit down, rest.

· ·

For your journal

How does this picture of a bench and the idea of sitting on it with Jesus make you feel?

What things in your life distract you or hold you back from spending time alone with Jesus?

What do you find hard about making time with Jesus and what could you do to make it easier?

The art of firewalking

Sooner or later, we come to a part of life that feels like walking through fire: bereavement, losing a job, miscarriage, illness or other difficult circumstances. Perhaps you're in the midst of a 'fire' time right now.

It's not so long since I came through a furnace of my own: moving from England to a new, less secure life overseas, dealing with my kids' reactions to leaving friends, coping with their heartache as well as my own. But, like Shadrach, Meshach and Abednego, thrown into a furnace because of their faithfulness to God, I have found his presence in it all.

In the story (Daniel 3) we're told that this furnace was made seven times hotter than usual. The miracle was not that the fire turned out not to be so hot after all – and moving country didn't turn out to be easier for me than I expected. But, like Shadrach, Meshach and Abednego, I walked out the other side eventually and, when I did, I discovered that I wasn't singed. Changed by the experience, certainly, but not scarred, not defeated, not destroyed.

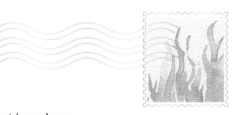

I now notice that the only things that have been burned away are ties that had bound me up: false beliefs and ways of living that had stopped me from being all that God wanted me to be. Now that's a miracle!

It's not that I believe that my heavenly Father caused the fire in my life. I've learned, though, that there are 'fire' times in life, and that when we choose to trust God and look for him among the flames, our wonderful, redemptive, creative Father can use them to bring us into new places of freedom.

Lord, be close.
When I walk into the fire,
hold me.
When all I see is flames,
let me turn to see your face.
On days when my failing heart cannot cry out to you,
Lord, please, call out to me.
Shout loud, whisper softly,
so I can lean towards your voice.
And until the day you lead me out into open space again,
let me know
that I am not alone.

For your journal

> If you want to travel with this idea a little more,
> read Isaiah 43:1–2. Write down how it makes you feel,
> to know that Jesus is with you even in the flames.

The Father's heart

Sometimes, a picture can speak to places so deep in our hearts that too many words might just get in the way.

This postcard is one of my all-time favourites.

I've struggled for most of my life as a Christian to relate to God as my father, especially in those times when I'm aware of how much I've messed things up. But this picture is both a declaration of the truth as I know it to be and an invitation to run into his love-filled, grace-soaked, judgement-free embrace.

If you too have ever struggled to call your heavenly
Father 'Abba' or 'Daddy', to accept his unconditional
love and embrace, maybe you should spend some
time with this postcard, asking him to take the truth
it represents and write it indelibly on your heart.

....

My child,

when your heart is hurt,
don't turn your face away;

when your soul is bruised,
don't break away and run;

when all you have to bring is shame,
don't find a place to hide.

Turn to me, run to me,
dive into my embrace
and find your rest in your Father's arms.

....

For your journal

Take a while to look at this postcard and write down what you feel God is saying to you through it. Have a go at writing your own poem, or write a letter back to God to capture what it means to you to be this child, to be welcomed and embraced by your 'Abba', to be unconditionally loved.

Changing key

I'm learning to play the piano... just enough to be able to accompany songs I like, using the chords written for guitar. I've got really good at songs written in the keys of C and D. I'm practised enough that when I see those chords, my hands can find them without me really having to think about it. The upshot is that I mostly play songs in those keys. If I'm just messing around for my own pleasure, I'll pick C or D; and if there's any danger that someone might hear me, I definitely stick to where I know I'm safe.

This morning, I felt that God said to me, 'You try to live your life in C and D.' Ouch! I guess I tend to live inside the boundaries of what I find comfortable.

I don't much like learning to play in a new key. It's slow and frustrating; it makes my hands ache and I have to keep thinking about what I'm trying to do.

But our heavenly Father wants us to persevere with the uncomfortable until it becomes natural – because all the time we are stretching out, covering more ground, we are pushing deeper into faith and adventure with him.

God wants to play a beautiful piece of music with your life. It's a duet, written by the great Creator to play alongside you, his precious child. It is awe-inspiring, extraordinary music, but it will only work if you're prepared to follow the key changes. You might have to follow him into stretching, uncomfortable places. You might have to work hard to keep up with him and you might long for your old comfortable, easy place. But then I didn't ever hear Jesus say, 'Come, follow me, and I will give you an easy, comfortable and unchallenging life'!

....

Jesus,
you are the one who goes ahead of me
and calls me out into new places.
Give me the courage to say
today,
'Yes. I will follow you.'

....

For your journal

> *What places are uncomfortable or comfortable for you?*
> *Ask Jesus to show you where he would take you if you*
> *were prepared to be stretched. Ask him to show you*
> *how he would care for you in that place.*

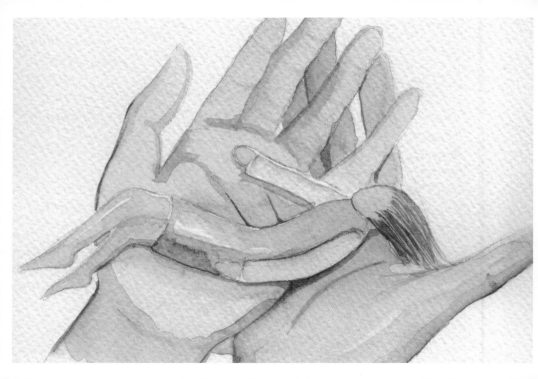

More than you can handle?

'God will never give you more than you can handle.'

This well-meant little piece of not-actually-scripture is, I'll admit, one of my 'pet peeves'. It annoys me because it seems to be saying that, whatever difficult or awful circumstance you might be walking through, you ought to be able to bear it alone, stoically. It also suggests that strength is to be rewarded with pain, more strength with more pain.

Pain and suffering are a part of life. Jesus never said that they wouldn't be (rather, the opposite). But I know many people who, even as I'm writing this, are in the middle of circumstances – financial, physical, emotional – that no one should be expected to be able to 'handle'. I know that some of them desperately need to have permission to 'not handle' it alone, so that they can be free to cry, shout, rest, lean on others and, above all, lean on the God who loves them.

Here's what I think is true:

Sometimes it's OK to say to God your Father, 'I can't handle this – I need you to step in with a miracle.' And this picture of a falling doll being caught safely in the father's hands is meant to show something of what I think our Father says to us in reply.

'I don't promise that
you won't have more in your life
than you can handle,
but I do promise that when you realise you can't handle it alone,
I *will* catch you.'

For your journal

: *What things in your life are hard to handle? What keeps*
: *you from letting go of your need to handle them alone?*

Name tapes

It's more than ten years since my firstborn started school. I still remember battling through the pile of freshly bought school uniform, sewing in the white woven name tapes, when my little boy came to ask me what I was doing.

Now, I've read that the average four-year-old asks around 200 questions a day, and mine was a bit above average in this department. So I cast around for an answer that would pre-empt further questions and send him back to his toys.

'I'm sewing in these name tapes to show everyone that the clothes belong to you, so that no one can take them away from you and they can't get lost.'

He looked thoughtful and then disappeared upstairs to his room. A minute later, he reappeared, dragging his much beloved Blue-Blanky. This worn and grubby cot blanket had been at his side for the past three years and was a great source of comfort to him.

'Sew my name on Blue-Blanky, Mummy,' he said earnestly. 'Then everyone will know it's mine, and and it can never ever be lost or taken away.' So I did.

About a week later I was reading Ephesians when this verse caught hold of my heart:

When you believed, you were marked in him with a seal, the promised Holy Spirit, who is a deposit guaranteeing our inheritance until the redemption of those who are God's possession – to the praise of his glory (Ephesians 1:13–14).

I suddenly realised that the Father has done the equivalent of sewing a name tape on to my heart and soul: he has marked me with a seal.

••

Isn't it wonderful? The Holy Spirit is the irrevocable royal seal on your life that declares to the earth and to the heavens for ever and ever, 'This soul is mine.'

When I look at this picture, I hear God whispering, 'Everyone will know you are mine; no one can say you are not, and you can never ever be lost or taken away.'

I wonder if you hear that, too?

••

For your journal

Sometimes beautiful truths like these hit up against a barrier of beliefs that we've taken on through other experiences. Ask God today to make this assurance real for you, and write down the way it makes you feel to belong to him like this.

Consider the birds

Have you ever noticed that when you sprinkle seed on to a bird table, in no time at all, loads of birds show up? I always find myself wondering, 'How on earth did they know?'

It turns out that lots of other people have asked this question too, and, although there's no definitive answer, two theories seem to emerge:

Birds have great eyesight and they're constantly watching for food; birds let each other know when they find something good and plentiful.

As I thought about this, I wondered what it meant for me as a follower of Jesus to be 'constantly watching for food'.

'Food' is anything that sustains you and helps you grow. So it could mean teaching, wisdom, reading the Bible, praying or worshipping with friends, or escaping to somewhere quiet to be alone with God. You might find it at certain times or places, in a person, at a prayer meeting, on the internet or in a book.

I think that God is calling me to be like a bird – an opportunistic feeder.

Birds will return to a place where they've been fed before, but will always be on the look-out for more. They are picky about what they will eat, but choose a variety of sources. This speaks to me about flexibility, alertness and also my own responsibility to seek God's provision for me. For a bird, maturity means to go out there and look for your own nutrition… not to stay where you are and wait to be fed.

···
I also wonder: how can I tell others about the feast?

Some birds form a community and let each other know where food can be found… by tweeting! It's easier to find out where to eat, how to grow, when we are part of a community.

Whether it's sharing a link on social media, sending a note, recommending a book or writing one, we all have a part to play in showing others where the food is. Helping others to get spiritually fed is a part of what we are called to do.

'Taste and see that the Lord is good' (Psalm 34:8).

···

For your journal

Think about the ways and places you 'find food'.

How can you pay more attention to these opportunities, or how could you look for new food sources?

How can you let others know about the feasts you find? Who in your life could you 'tweet' to?

A fast car and a plastic ballerina

This week I was reading again that one of the keys to experiencing God's presence in our lives is to be hungry for him. While a big part of me said, 'Yes, yes, yes', a small but significant part said, 'But I'm so-o-o-o tired, I just don't have the energy to get more hungry!'

And then God reminded me about the plastic ballerina and the Aston Martin…

I saw the car in a showroom when we were trying to choose a boring family hatchback. Until that moment I'd only cared that we found something clean, reliable and with enough luggage space for a travel cot and a double buggy. Then I saw a gorgeous dark blue convertible Aston Martin... and I wanted it!

Of course, we couldn't afford it; there was no space for the pushchairs and small sticky fingers would have ruined the upholstery. But it was beautiful, and as I looked at it, desire bubbled up in my heart.

The plastic ballerina lived in a pink jewellery box belonging to my cousin. When I was about six I went to visit and was entranced by the spinning figure and the tinkly music. I wanted it so badly, it almost hurt.

God used these pictures to remind me that hunger for him isn't something I have to dredge up from somewhere. It's not reliant on my own effort. I didn't try to get hungry for the Aston Martin or the plastic ballerina. When you spend time looking at something beautiful, imagining having it in your life – hunger rises up, all by itself.

65

....

Father, show me
a glimpse of your Son –
expose a fragment of his beauty,
uncover a corner of the mystery,
reveal a fraction of his glory
to my eyes –
and take my heart captive once again.

....

For your journal

Would you like to hunger for God more?

This week, spend some time looking at Jesus. Read parts of the Gospels, write a list of all the things he has already done in your life, or all the things that you've heard him say to you. Look for him where he is already at work in your life and dream the dreams of how life could be with more of his presence in it…

Don't stress about it. As you gaze on his beauty, the hunger for more of him will just rise up. Blessed are those who are hungry!

Immeasurably more...

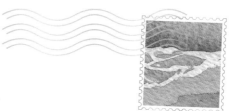

There's something awkward about asking for more... and that awkwardness often stops me from asking.

To be clear, I'm not talking about material wealth, although for many people it may be reasonable to ask for more of that. I'm thinking about other things I'd like more of: faith, wisdom, passion, courage, forgiveness, healing, ability to receive God's love, love for others, a sense of the presence of God...

But for some reason I find that coming to God and saying, 'Please, I want more' is really difficult.

Asking for more when I have already received so much from God feels greedy. But for each of us, the truth is that God has more to give us – more understanding, more faith, more peace, more of his presence, more love. And his pockets don't hold a limited amount: if he gives to me, it doesn't mean that someone else will miss out!

Every time I stand on the beach I scoop up as much water as I can hold in my hands and I think, 'This is how much of God's presence, power and peace I have experienced so far.' Then I look out at the sea.

The difference between the water I can hold in my hands and the contents of the Mediterranean Sea (and then the Atlantic Ocean) is beyond my ability to comprehend. That's how much more there is to explore of God; that's how much more he has for you.

You just need to ask.

I pray that out of his glorious riches he may strengthen you with power through his Spirit in your inner being, so that Christ may dwell in your hearts through faith. And I pray that you, being rooted and established in love, may have power, together with all the Lord's holy people, to grasp how wide and long and high and deep is the love of Christ, and to know this love that surpasses knowledge – that you may be filled to the measure of all the fullness of God.

Now to him who is able to do immeasurably more than all we ask or imagine, according to his power that is at work within us, to him be glory in the church and in Christ Jesus throughout all generations, for ever and ever! Amen.

Ephesians 3:16–21

For your journal

- *What do you want to ask God for 'more' of?*
- *What stops you from asking? Ask today!*

How God moves

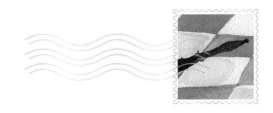

OK, I'll admit it: God doesn't always act the way I expect him to. His timing can be wonderful but sometimes it can be extremely frustrating.

It seems to me that in the kingdom of God there's a lot of waiting and a fair amount of 'suddenly'. And the suddenly stuff would often fit neatly under the heading of 'not quite what I expected'. We often expect our progress towards the things God has promised us to be step by step in a straightforward direction, like the pawn on a chessboard. But perhaps it's more normal to be a bishop!

Each type of chess piece has its own unique way of moving. Pawns usually take one step forward at a time, while the bishops can move right across the board, diagonally, in one move. They may spend the early part of the game not moving at all, but can zoom from the back to the thick of the battle in an instant.

So I've painted a chess bishop for all those waiting on the back row, wondering when God will use them and how. It's for those who have heard God's call to do something, and yearn for a step-by-step route to get there, but don't see the 'pieces' falling into place.

I hate waiting. Patience is a spiritual fruit I'm yet to grow much of. But I know that I shouldn't abandon God's promises for me and my family just because his timing is not what I'd expected. So, when I am trying to work out how God could possibly fulfil his promises to me, I'm learning to remember that walking his way may not be step by step in a straight line. It might involve some 'suddenly'.

Waiting impatiently
for a moment in battle,
unwillingly
hidden away

struggling painfully
with unresolved promises,
fighting to hear
what you say

desperately hoping
I've not been forgotten,
fearfully wondering why?

and then suddenly…

For your journal

- Meditate on and pray through Psalm 40:1–3 or
  write down a list of the things God has promised
  you and ask him to help you wait for them in faith.

Climbing the helter-skelter

This is the kind of helter-skelter I remember from when I was a child. We would pick up a rather dubious-smelling sack, go inside the tower and climb a spiral staircase for what seemed like for ever. Eventually, legs aching, we arrived at the top and stepped out into the daylight, ready for the exhilaration of the ride down, feeling giddy as we looked back down at where we'd come from.

I remembered that feeling when I read a blog post written by an old friend, someone with whom I used to walk to school, giggling about boys and exchanging make-up tips – who one day, about 26 years ago, stood next to me as we both whispered 'yes' to Jesus and fell into his never-ending grace.

My friend wrote honestly about years of fighting anxiety, choosing to trust God when she wanted to run. She wrote about a 'stepping out' moment, when she should have been terrified but realised that she had learned to lean into God, to walk without fear.

Life often feels like the helter-skelter. We can live for many uncomfortable years in the darkness of not really being sure what God is doing. We climb onwards and upwards, with only little glimpses – hope – of where we're going or what we might be achieving. Sometimes we feel as if we're moving in a circle, continually returning to familiar places of pain, weakness or battle.

••

The challenge is not to give up... because, as we circle around, revisiting old issues and fighting similar battles, and as we press into God and call out to him, we are actually spiralling upwards to higher places.

It's not easy going, but it is going somewhere – and we can look forward to the time when we emerge into the daylight and realise that the old battles have at last been won.

••

For your journal

Be honest with yourself and with God about the 'sacks' that you are carrying. What are the places that you seem to come back to over and over again? What lesson is taking you a long time to learn?

Ask God to give you a glimpse of what it will be like to ride free in the blessing of the freedom you've earned. How will you live, how will you feel, and what will you do differently?

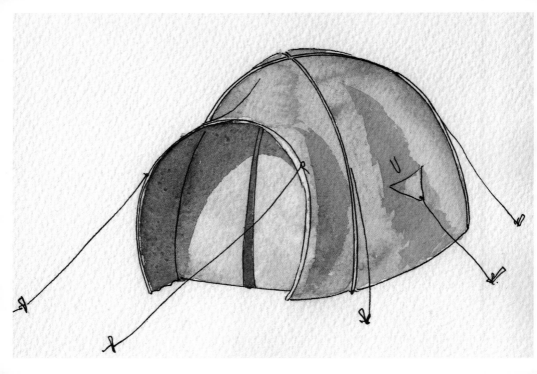

There's no place like home

My family are summer nomads. Once a year we leave the summer heat of Cyprus and head for the UK, where we live out of (several) suitcases for five fun, but long, weeks.

Sleeping in a tent or the guest beds of friends and family is wonderful. But about three weeks in, a longing rises up to pop home for a few days, run the washing machine ten times, sleep in my own bed and then go back to England to spend more time with the friends I love.

It's reminded me of Paul describing our bodies
as 'tents' (in 2 Corinthians 5:1), temporary
accommodation, to be replaced one day by a
'permanent building' in heaven. And in Paul's day,
tents weren't for weekend leisure-campers. They
were for people who, for a long time or a short time,
were living on the move.

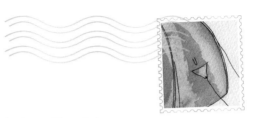

I wonder whether my earthly life is, in reality, a lot like my family's summer trip back to the UK. Maybe the point is not to get too comfortable or settled, but to do (and enjoy) those things that won't be possible in heaven... seeking the lost, telling God's story, loving the outcasts, defending the oppressed, caring for those in need.

Perhaps we are just 'temporary nomads' in the world for a while before we head back to our actual home with God (in a refreshed and renewed earth).

••

Long-term travelling and camping is fun but not easy. It can be uncomfortable, difficult and inconvenient – but it's also an opportunity. It's too big an opportunity to waste on feeling homesick and complaining about feeling unsettled.

Our lives, like each and every summer, will eventually come to an end. Like every airport departure we make, there will be tearful goodbyes and regrets about what we didn't get done, but it will be OK... we'll be going home.

••

For your journal

∶ *How do you feel when you sense God calling you*
∶ *to move on for him, to leave a settled life?*

Thirsty?

I know that in the heat of summer, especially in hotter countries, it is very important to drink lots of water. But I am the sort of person who gets busy and caught up in things, and I often just forget.

I've noticed that when I've gone a long time without drinking and am feeling thirsty, I take a while to realise what the problem is. I sometimes even try other things – an apple, a biscuit – not recognising what it is that my body is craving.

Sometimes we can feel like this about spending time alone with Jesus. We forget how much we need him, how much his presence is like water to our souls, and we become 'spiritually dehydrated' without noticing. And yet, as when our bodies need water, one taste of pure refreshing time with Jesus can be enough to reawaken our thirst and make us drink long and deep.

Perhaps you too have been busy and distracted? Perhaps you have not noticed how thirsty your soul has become? Why not come now and take a sip? Ask your loving Father to pour his refreshing Spirit over your soul. Sit with him for a while, and enjoy the precious refreshment he longs to bring you.

Holy Spirit, come;
drip living water
on to my lips
and, as I drink,
bring streams of sweet refreshment
into the thirsty land
that is my soul.
Reawaken my thirst for you,
until I cry out for more
and more
and more,
and then let me be
soaked in you
day after day, year after year,
so that I never thirst again.

For your journal

How might you become spiritually dried out
without noticing? What are the practices or
disciplines that help you to press in to God?
What new ones could you try?

Fuchsia and bindweed

Even after many years living in the grace of being a Christian, I often look at the piles of rubbish (stupid beliefs, insecurities, hurts, weaknesses and sin) in my life and think, 'Come on, Lord, why can't you just sort me out quicker?'

I painted this picture during a healing conference, when I was going over old ground again, especially the need to forgive and accept forgiveness.
I was feeling frustrated that there seemed to be more 'junk' to deal with. But in the middle of that frustration God reminded me of this picture.

When we were first married, we lived in a house with a beautiful pink and purple fuchsia in the front garden. I'm not a great gardener, but I once spent a whole afternoon tending to this plant. Bindweed had grown up all over it, spiralling around every branch and stem until the whole shrub was weighed down by the weed.

I was desperate to save it, but ripping at the weed would certainly have destroyed my lovely fuchsia. So I had no choice but to sit and slowly unwrap it, leaf by leaf, stem by stem. It took a long time.

God showed me that I am like the fuchsia – delicate, beautiful, cherished – and that he is like a gardener – careful, deliberate, patient and thorough. I have no doubt that my powerful Father could heal me quickly, could tear out all the parts of me that are marred and broken, twisted up or distorted. But his desire is not simply to get rid of the weed but to save the plant and see it restored.

'Heal me,' I said.
'Heal me quickly, Lord.'
'I'll do it carefully,' he replied,
'so that all that is wonderful,
all that is beautiful,
all that I cherish so much
in you
will remain.'

For your journal

Do you ever feel impatient with God when he is slow to heal you? Ask him to help you adjust to his timing. Write down all the ways in which you have seen him heal you in the past and give thanks to him for the journey he has brought you on so far.

My boy's dream car

This push-along-with-your feet-car was the object of desire of every single child at the toddler group. My son wanted to ride in it long before his legs were long enough or coordinated enough to be able to move it himself. And I still can't see one of these red and yellow beauties without smiling at the thought of him as a three-year-old, chubby-cheeked and grinning as he trundled around the yard.

For a while, this was his ultimate dream car.

Now he is 15, with the same wild blond hair and cheeky grin, but they now top a nearly six-foot-tall body. I'm not sure it would even be possible for him to fold his gangly frame into this little car, much less move it anywhere.

This picture speaks to me about hopes and dreams. When I was 20, I dreamed of travelling, having a family, helping people find Jesus, healing, preaching, leading worship, seeing revival… Some of it has happened, some hasn't; and there's also been lots of amazing, difficult, wonderful stuff that I didn't expect.

These days, I tend to think of crazy hopeful dreaming as something that young people do. It's tempting to put those dreams down and just get on with life the way it is… but I think God wants us to continue having dreams.

The dreams will change, though. This trundly little car was a toddler's dream. It was a great dream for my son to have when he was three… but now it is totally outgrown, utterly unsuitable. He needs to get a bigger dream.

Do you still have dreams about what God might do with your life? Maybe you've lost hold of them on the rollercoaster of life. Maybe you've forgotten what they even were. Never mind, you've probably outgrown them anyway.

Today is a good day to ask God to give you a new dream, a new vision of what he wants to do with you and in you and through you.

For your journal

> When you ask God about what dreams he has
> for your life today, write down what he says.

Rooted

'May your roots go down deep into the soil of God's marvellous love' (Ephesians 3:17, Living Bible).

I keep coming back to wondering how to send roots down deeper and deeper into God's love, because I love this picture of a tree. It's a bit like the one described in Jeremiah 17:8, which is fruitful in every season and circumstance. It has a root system that goes deep into the water table, so that even when there's no water to be seen on the surface, it's able to draw refreshment and life up from those deep places.

My spiritual life seems to run in seasons. Sometimes I'm flying: Jesus has never seemed so close, and every page of the Bible comes alive. A few months later, everything suddenly seems much more difficult. For a long while I thought this was a kind of malfunction, but I'm starting to believe it might not be so abnormal. All around us, seasons come and go; plants grow vigorously and are then pruned back; people are active and then sleep. It seems to be the way of the world that our Father has created – things have a rhythm to them.

The picture of being rooted says to me that perhaps it's OK for spiritual life to be seasonal, but it is possible to be rooted in God's love in such a way that no matter what season you are in, living water can always be drawn up from the deep.

Are you in an easy season or a dry one? Are storm winds catching your branches or are you resting in a time of peace? Either way, the advice is the same: send your roots down deeper into the river of life.

··

Plant me, Lord,
on the bank of a river.
Show me how to send roots deep into you,
so that in good years,
in bad years,
in wet times and in dry,
there will be fruit to feed the hungry.
There will be leaves to give shelter to the weary.
There will be the promise of water for the thirsty.
And when the storm comes, though I bend in the force of the wind,
my heart will remain, anchored to yours,
like a tree planted by the water.

··

For your journal

How would you describe the season you are in? What ways do you have to send your roots deep? How can you plan to have more space for 'root growing' in your life? If this is something you struggle with, who could you ask for help, so that you can learn from their experience?

Pray first

Have you ever tried cutting fabric with children's paper scissors? It can be done, but would be very difficult. With short, blunt blades it's likely to be time consuming, and you could only take short snips (or hacks). Chances are, your line will end up ragged and wonky. The fabric might even be ruined.

What a difference it makes to use my special dressmaking scissors (woe betide anyone who 'borrows' them to cut paper!). These are large, sharp as can be and heavy enough to take some of the hard work out of cutting even thick fabrics.

As I was painting this postcard, I felt God say to me that every job I do without taking time to pray first is like trying to cut fabric with paper scissors. Sometimes they will be enough and I'll struggle through. I might not do a brilliant job but it will be OK. Sometimes, though, it will be all but impossible. I will give up, frustrated and exhausted by the task.

But if I ask, the Holy Spirit can transform my 'enough', my little scissors, into dressmakers' shears that can cut easily, fast and well. Prayer makes that kind of difference: it can make the difficult easy and the impossible achievable.

I can keep going (with my little paper scissors) and face every challenge all by myself, but *why would I choose to make my life that difficult?*

....

Remember these two little words. They are transforming my week and can transform yours, too. 'Pray first.'

....

For your journal

Make a list of all you have to do today (or this week) which may prove difficult, or take effort, or need careful handling. Pray through the list and ask God for his help and insight in each case.

Gappiness

This is my beautiful nearly-six-year-old's new smile. Gorgeous, isn't it?

I'll admit, though, that when she ran to me yesterday, yelling with excitement that the wobbly front tooth was finally out, I did have a little moment of grieving for that pearly-toothed little-girl smile that I will never see again.

And then, before I knew it, I was wondering what her big teeth will be like. Will they come through straight and strong? Will they look too big for a while in her mouth? Will she still look like my little girl?

I was stuck there for a moment in an emotional whirlwind, caught up between grief over what has been lost and anxiety about what is ahead...

Then she smiled!

And I heard God whisper, 'Gappiness is just so beautiful, isn't it?'

And it is...

When I was an architecture student, we studied liminal spaces: corridors, walkways, vestibules, porches, thresholds. We talked about how important it is to help people realise that they are making a transition, preparing them for the next space.

I remember all that as I see people passing through liminal life-spaces, between what was and what will be, travelling the 'gappiness'. We need to see these liminal spaces as temporary places of rest, gaps where God can prepare us for the next season. They may seem awkward, but they have their own beauty.

My girl showed me this morning that she can just see the tip of the new tooth poking through. Before I know it, she will have her big-teeth smile, but it will take a while, and for now I'm going to lean back and enjoy the gappiness.

For your journal

*Can you remember any liminal, in-between times
in your life? How did you travel them? What beauty
could you see in them? What advice could you give to
yourself to help you travel them better the next time?*

Walking on the water

I've always loved the story of Peter leaping
enthusiastically out of the boat and walking towards
Jesus across the water. Over the years I've thought
about it a lot as I've tried hard to have the guts
to follow Jesus into the places he's called me to.
There are probably a hundred different important,
challenging lessons you could find in this story, but
I'm picking the three that I've been thinking about
recently. Maybe God will speak to you through one
of them…

First, the other people in the boat were possibly not shouting, 'Go, Peter!' I wonder whether the other disciples heard Jesus' voice above the waves. If not, then their reaction would almost certainly have been of the 'Where are you going, you nutter?' variety.

Sometimes God speaks to us through our peers, often through our leaders, and always in line with the Bible; but occasionally he calls us to do something that looks kind of crazy to a lot of people...

Second, Peter only went where he was called to go.

He heard Jesus and obeyed, even though it looked and felt impossible. Note that he didn't just wildly do something that looked impossible and then ask Jesus to bless him in it. There's a big difference…

Third, 'safe' is relative. I'm not into taking risks. Unlike my own little girl, I have an inner drive to stay safe. I've heard a lot of talks about walking on water that suggest it's about taking risks, stepping out of the safety of the boat. But that misses an interesting question: 'Where do you think is safer? In the boat or where Jesus is?'

••

I guess it depends a bit on your definition of 'safe', but I'm inclined to wonder whether, in that moment, Peter saw the boat for what it was, and Jesus for who he was. He really didn't want to leave the comfort of a safe, predictable boat, but he really wanted to walk on water, and he couldn't have it both ways.

That's my prayer for today – for a yearning to replace comfort with courage, to go beyond the limits of my fragile faith, to walk on water.

••

For your journal

If you want to walk on water in your life with God, the first step is being able to hear him when he calls to you. Invest some time in finding out how to do that. Make some time to listen to him today, about the things you're already doing, and maybe make some space for him to call you out of the boat again.

When climbing a mountain

Intrigued? I'm not surprised! I didn't know what one of these was, either. It's a piton. Mountain climbers hammer them into crevices in the rock so that they can attach their safety ropes through the hole. It's a vital piece of climbing kit.

When God showed me this picture, I imagined what it would be like if, exhausted from a difficult climb, you were to come across one of these, already firmly in the rock face and ready to clip your harness on to. What a relief it would be! I would feel so grateful to the climber who had left it for me to take hold of.

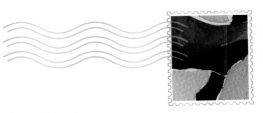

So today's postcard is an encouragement to start nailing in some of these beauties, both for those who scale the rockface after you and for your own benefit (in case, like me, you have a tendency to revisit the same challenges).

Our faith in God is like that: we can hold it out to others and say, 'Here, hold on to mine, I've scaled this rock before you.' While a piton has to be strong, the real strength is in the rock. The job of the piton is simply to enable someone to anchor their heart to the Rock of Ages, into the strength of the living God.

I can't tell you exactly what the pitons that you hammer in will look like. They might be a word of knowledge, an action, a scripture passage glued to a mirror, a testimony, a song, a journal entry, a book, a blog post, a status update or a tweet. But I do know that when we start to hold out to others the faith we've gathered, it will multiply. Whatever they say about problems, faith shared is faith (at least) doubled.

••

If you're climbing in some kind of storm, look out for what others have left for you. When you see it, reach out for it and clip yourself on.

If you've taken on a difficult rock face and made it to the top, celebrate that moment. Then look for the faith that grew in you on the journey and find a way to hold it out so that others can climb after you.

••

For your journal

- *What mountains have you climbed in your life with*
- *God? What mountains do you face? In what places*
- *could you look for testimony that you can clip your*
- *faith on to? How can you share your own testimony*
- *of God's faithfulness?*

Clean water

The city I live in has a long-term problem. The water pipes supplying the outlying villages have decayed and started releasing something toxic into the water. It's not clear how long the problem will take to fix, but no one will want to drink that water until then.

God has been speaking to me through this about the importance of keeping our 'water supply' pure, because the fountain of water that he has placed in each of us that choose to follow him is not just for ourselves but also for all those around us.

In case you haven't realised it yet, you are not just a kitchen tap; you're a public water fountain. It's part of Jesus' crazy, wonderful, upside-down, revolutionary economy that when someone comes to him, thirsty and asking for a drink, he makes them into a spring.

That in itself is amazing, but what the Nicosia Water Board's problems have been whispering to me lately is this: 'The pipes matter.'

I'm feeling challenged this week because our dodgy water supply has reminded me that any bitterness, unforgiveness, cynicism or hatred in my heart will pollute the water that flows out from me in my friendships, my relationships and ministry. If I don't want to have these things in my heart slowly leaching toxic waste into the people around me, then I need to do something about them.

All you amazing, extraordinary, wonderful fountains of living water reading this postcard, it's time for us all to get cleaned up. There's a world full of thirsty people out there and it's time to give them a drink.

'Whoever believes in me, as Scripture has said, rivers of living water will flow from within them' (John 7:38).

For your journal

Ask God to show you if there's anything in your heart that could pollute the water you are giving out to others. Is there unforgiveness or bitterness that could make the water less fresh? Is there any blockage of fear or self-hatred that could be preventing you from sharing your living water with others? If he reveals anything, ask for his forgiveness and receive it.

Emerging

Every now and again, something happens in your heart or your life that is so significant, so major, that you know nothing will ever be quite the same again.

Sometimes, in just a few days or moments, your life can become so different that for a while you find yourself out of step with the rest of the world. 'How can everyone else's life still be so much the same when mine has changed so radically?' you ask yourself.

I can think of seven moments in my life when I felt this kind of thing really powerfully: asking Jesus to be a part of my life, getting married, the births of each of my three children, a miscarriage and then the death of my dad. All these things so profoundly affected me on the inside that I struggled to understand why people around me couldn't sense or be a part of the revolution that had taken place. I felt a bit detached from the rest of the world for a while, and I didn't always give myself the grace that I needed to process these moments.

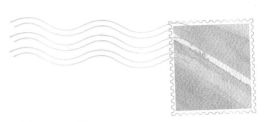

The Monarch Butterfly, after hatching out of its cocoon, sits for an hour or more in the sun, allowing its wings to dry and become strong. And this moment of rest, warming and taking stock speaks to me powerfully.

So often, I experience a revolution in my life and I expect myself to be up and out and flying straight away. I think Jesus is reminding me that I can wait a while, let my wings dry out and get used to my new shape. I can rest in him for a moment or two before I launch out again.

Imagine my surprise
when I emerge from the struggle –
the beautiful revolution,
the inner rewriting –
with wings.

Still reeling
but knowing
that one day soon I will stretch out
into what I've become,
and fly.

But till then
I'll sit here
in the light and the warmth of your gaze
and let you tell me again
who I am.

For your journal

If you're not in this place right now, store up the thought for the future. Decide now that, if and when it happens, you will give yourself permission to rest and to ask God to shine his light on your wings.

If you are in this place, go easy on yourself. Write a letter to God about the change that you've just been through. Take a moment to say goodbye to what you were before and stretch out into the new thing you've become. Absorb the light of God's presence in whatever way works best for you right now. Be blessed.

Also from BRF

Believe in Miracles

A spiritual journey of positive change

Carmel Thomason

Believe in Miracles is a 40-day journey into a world of possibility. Focusing on small practical steps, you are invited to follow a series of short exercises that will help bring about lasting changes in your life, leading to a more prayerful, contented and connected state of being. By looking for the good and focusing on actions to take now, you will learn to view differently your daily circumstances, your relationship with God, and your relationships with others, bringing something of the ways of heaven to earth.

ISBN 978 0 85746 420 0   £8.99
Available from your local Christian bookshop or direct from BRF: please visit www.brfonline.org.uk

Moments of Grace

Reflections on meeting with God

Joy MacCormick

From desolation to celebration, loneliness to love, *Moments of Grace* offers pithy, thought-provoking reflections on themes connecting God, faith and the journey of life. Questions for further pondering help the reader make links between head and heart, between what they believe, what they wrestle with believing and what they experience day by day.

Joy MacCormick has written this book to help people have a closer encounter with God in prayer, especially those who may struggle to find a place in conventional church worship.

ISBN 978 0 85746 224 4   £6.99
Available from your local Christian bookshop or direct from BRF: please visit www.brfonline.org.uk

Journalling the Bible

40 writing exercises

Corin Child

The spiritual discipline of journalling has become increasingly popular in recent years and this book shows how it can furitfully overlap with creative writing to provide an original way of engaging with the Bible.

'Bible study' is usually taken to mean 'reading and discussing', but writing offers a different way of interacting with the text, generating new insights and application even from the most familiar of passages. Journalling the Bible offers 40 writing/ journalling exercises that have been tested in workshops around the country, providing an imaginative resource for individual and group work.

ISBN 978 1 84101 736 5   £7.99
Available from your local Christian bookshop or direct from BRF: please visit www.brfonline.org.uk

Also from BRF

The Contemplative Minister

Learning to lead from the still centre

Ian Cowley

At one time Christian ministry offered the opportunity to spend your life in the study of God's word, reading and reflection, prayer and sermon preparation, and the faithful pastoral care of a community. These days there are very few jobs in full-time ministry which do not require a heroic combination of stamina, multi-tasking and change management. Drawing on his experience of developing and leading relevant training programmes, Ian Cowley assesses the stresses and pressures of the job and shows how to grow into a 'contemplative minister', prioritising a relationship of deepening love with God.

ISBN 978 0 85746 360 9   £8.99
Available from your local Christian bookshop or direct from BRF: please visit
www.brfonline.org.uk.

Working from a Place of Rest

Jesus and the key to sustaining ministry

Tony Horsfall

Exhaustion, burnout, tiredness, even breakdown… sadly, such conditions are all too common these days, not least among those involved in some kind of Christian ministry. Drawing on extensive experience of training and mentoring across the world, Tony Horsfall reflects on the story of Jesus and the Samaritan woman to draw out practical guidance for sustainable Christian life and work. As he writes: 'Come and sit by the well for a while. Watch Jesus and see how he does it. Listen to what the Spirit may be saying to you deep within; and maybe God will give you some insights that will change your life.'

ISBN 978 1 84101 544 6   £6.99
Available from your local Christian bookshop or direct from BRF: please visit www.brfonline.org.uk.

Dust and Glory

Daily Bible readings from Ash Wednesday to Easter Day

David Runcorn

During Lent, the church calls us to a special period of prayer, self-examination and teaching—and this book has been written to accompany you through that period. *Dust and Glory* aims to draw us to authentic faith—a way of living and believing that is real and vulnerable, strong in knowing its limits, rooted in joy and wonder, blessed with the healing and merciful presence of God. Such faith acknowledges both the dust of our mortality and the glory that keeps breaking in with unexpected life, hope and new beginnings.

ISBN 978 0 85746 357 9   £7.99
Available from your local Christian bookshop or direct from BRF: please visit www.brfonline.org.uk.